MYOPIA

Poems By

Pamela Martin

Myopia
Copyright 2008 by Pamela Gowan

All rights reserved under International and Pan-American copyright conventions. No part of this book may be reproduced, stored in a retrieval system or transmitted in any form, electronic, mechanical, or by any other means, without written permission of the author.

International Standard Book Number: 978-0-615-26437-0

Illustrated by Kathleen Hardy.

Table of Contents

Part I

On the Brink	9
The Windy City	9
Death Be Not Proud	9
Pro se	10
Blessed Redeemer	10
Bingo Jingo	10
Earning His Keep	11
Better Than Nothing	12
Denotation	12
Self-Abasement	12
Rolls Royce	13
"WE TH P PUL"	14
Stock Quotes	14
Pilgrim's Progress	14
Selfish Gene	15
Charlatan	16
Justice, U.S.A.	16
Sui generis	*16*
Flatus	17
"Get with the Program"	18
The Afterglow	18
Ode Records	18
Paranoid Prayer	19
Cultural Litteracy	20
A Metaphor for Life	20
Stockholm syndrome	20
Sacerdotal Privilege	21
The Hereafter	21
Vanitas vanitatum	21
Probity	22
Attenuation	22
Hearsay	22
"For You"	23
Playing Hooky	23
Flippant	23

Part II

Defiance 27
Desperado 27
Recherche 27
Ambivalence 28
Chastisements 28
Superficialities.. 28
"The Florida Foot".. 29
Pennies from Heaven 30
Insouciance 30
Taedium vitae 30
The Judgment of Paris 31
Atonement.. 32
A Lethal Combination 32
Recent History 32
Sotheby's.. 33
Work in Progress 34
Sunday Mourning... 34
Encyclical... 34
Apnea!... 35
Neverland 36
Cheat Sheet 36
Gabriel.. 36
Osteoporosis... 37
The Assignation 38
Rendezvous 38
Always, Sometimes, Never.. 38
Deceit and Deception 39
Spousal Privilege 39
The Hanoverian Regression 39
Bragging Rites 40
Flying Solo 40
Elysian Fields... 40
Love Lingers 41
Quatrain.. 41
Captains Courageous 41

Part III

Solicitude 45
The Rapture 45
Penny-wise 45
Insecurity 46
Identity 46
Manumission 46
Water Proof 47
On the Rebound 48
Cupbearer 48
At the Rainbow's End 48
Catalyst 49
Freedom 50
The Good Die Young. 50
BlackBerry Jam 50
Myopia 51
Reality Check 52
A Diet of Worms 52
INRI 52
"Rivet" 53
Taking That First Step 54
Chanson de geste 54
Pacifism 54
Chick Flick 55
Horace Greedy 56
W.C.T.U. 56
Swansong 56
Urban Legend 57
Renal Failure 57
Persiflage 57
Maxima propositio 58
Sylvan 58
Hog Wash 58
Darwinism 59
B.F.F. 59
He Who Hesitates is Lost. 59

Part I

On the Brink

He took her to the precipice.
She had been before.
He told her it was just a cliff.
The rain began to pour.
He reached out and took her hand
And called, "Sweet, Emily."
The Belle of Amherst spoke at last:
"Death is mine enemy."

The Windy City

Change is good.
Change is great.
Change is something
To celebrate!
Change is as constant
As the wind
That blows so gently
On the skin.

Death Be Not Proud

I could not say it better.
It could not be more clear.
No lifetime is sufficient
To allay our fears
Of permanent separation
From someone we hold dear.
I shudder at the thought.
The end is drawing near.

*Pro se**

Judy is a judge
Who doesn't hold a grudge
And will not ever budge
On principle.
And she does not hesitate
To pontificate
On your legal fate
But is often risible.

*Latin for "represent oneself (in court)."

Blessed Redeemer

I'm a soldier of fortune,
A prisoner of fate.
But sometimes I wonder
If it's not too late
For the redemption
I know to be
Part of the birthright
He promised me.

Bingo Jingo

Bingo is my favorite sport.
I play it all the time.
We play it at St. Stephen's.
It really is divine.
Some folks think that it's a sin
But I dismiss their case.
Win, lose or draw.
It is no disgrace.

Earning His Keep

I was walking in the woods
One fine winter's day
When out jumped a rabbit
Who had no place to stay.
"You can stay with me," I said,
"I'll take care of you.
And I think you will make
Delicious rabbit stew."

Better Than Nothing

It was written in the stars.
We were meant to be.
You and me together
In my fantasy.
But if I can only have you
In my waking dreams,
It's better than nothing
Strange as it seems.

Denotation

A stoic and a cynic
Were walking hand in hand
Through the streets of Athens
Shooting rubber bands.
The stoic shot the cynic
Who looked him and said:
"You are so impassive,
And I am so jaded."

Self-abasement

We have been victorious
When God was on our side.
We have been vainglorious
When we had too much pride.
But we are humble in our origins.
We eat humble pie
Every hour of every day
No one can deny.

Rolls Royce

I was playing "air" drums
In the front seat of my car.
If I did not know better,
I could be a star.
But that doesn't matter.
I was on a roll.
Even Ringo Starr
Doesn't have more soul.

"WE TH P PUL"*

Stick it to the government
Every chance you get.
Have you noticed lately
What is your personal debt?
If you think that that's too high,
You are not alone.
And tell me have you lately
Paid your sub-prime loan?

*"We the People."

Stock Quotes

The truth is we may never know
The meaning of true love.
But we seek it anyway.
What is not to love?
Some say it is futile
To pursue this quest.
But I say, "Lead on, McDuff."
Father knows best.

Pilgrim's Progress

The time has come
For me to go.
But to where
I do not know.
Still I go there
Willingly
Because He has
Great plans for me.

Selfish Gene

In a solipsistic universe
There is only me.
In this lonely world,
You could never be.
Narcissism is a kind
Of selfish chemistry
That isolates the spirit
From its sociality.

Charlatan

An ounce of Pounce for you
Is a pound of cure for me.
It's better than think
As a basic remedy.
I do not indulge
In any quackery.
So, you can not go wrong
When you put your trust in me.

Justice, U.S.A.

Justice is a place
We will never know.
No matter how we try.
No matter where we go.
For justice can't be served
Internuncio
Unless it is blind
To who and what we know.

*Sui generis**

She's one in a 1,000,000.
She's one of a kind.
She's the purest of pleasures.
She's so refined.
They broke the mold
In which she was cast.
Life without her is
A life at half-mast.

*Latin for "without equal; unique."

Flatus

The time will come
When you will be
As pretty as
A lass can be.
But that time
Will come to pass
And soon you will be
Passing gas.

"Get With the Program"

To play the devil's advocate
Is to play the fool
Every hour of every day
As you have learned in school.
I daresay that to naysay
Subverts the golden rule.
So, just say "nay" to naysay
And end this ridicule.

The Afterglow

I took you home for just one drink.
Instead you spent the night.
But what a phantom you became
When I turned out the light.
I could not take my eyes off you.
It's as if you glowed.
Like the sun that burns so bright,
Your phosphorescence showed.

Ode Records

I sold my soul to rock & roll.
I made a bad deal.
No matter what you say or do
That's just how I feel.
From Elvis to Costello
Madonna to Sir Paul,
After all these years
I have heard it all.

Paranoid Prayer

May fortune smile upon you
And sunshine light your way
And hope spring eternal
Each and every day.
May peace be with you.
Sing with joy his praise.
May goodness and God's mercy
Follow you always.

Cultural Litteracy

"You had me at 'hello,'"
I told the operator.
"I am just a friend,"
I told the alligator.
A prisoner of love
Must have a liberator.
"Justice for all"
Must have an educator.

A Metaphor for Life

I took a roller coaster ride.
I fought back the tears.
I should have loosened up a bit.
I should have had a beer.
But sober is what I would be
Although I nearly died.
Life is but a roller coaster
Deep down inside.

Stockholm syndrome

I and my captor
Are one and the same.
When I was abducted,
I didn't complain.
When the time came,
I wouldn't go home.
Without my captor,
I feel alone.

Sacerdotal Privilege

I told the police, I would find peace
After I made confession.
They waited outside, then gave me a ride
To a place of detention.
They questioned the priest about the deceased
But all that he would tell 'em
Was he made a vow and is keeping it now
As written on the vellum.

The Hereafter

I have heard the end is near
As near as Armageddon.
The time has come for each of us
To come to Him and reckon.
We welcome Him with hearts of joy
And at times with laughter.
It matters not what came before
Only what comes after.

Vanitas vanitatum*

Vanity of vanities.
So says Ecclesiastes.
I sue you and you sue me.
The bonfire of the vanities.
Lovers come and lovers go.
Time is your greatest foe.
It will hang you out to dry
And give you not a reason why.

*Vulgate Bible, Ecclesiastes 1:2; *"Vanitas vanitatum, et omnia vanitas."*
(Vanity of vanities, all is vanity.)

Probity

Judy Miller was a pillar
Of society.
It came upon her to love and honor
All propriety.
She was blessed, we can attest,
With blissful irony
Which gave her hope that she could cope
With life's debauchery.

Attenuation

My doctor is a doctor
Whose patients wear him thin.
I can't help but wonder
What is wrong with him.
A little razzle-dazzle
Could only do him good
As he upholds the Hippocratic Oath
As best as best he could.

Hearsay

Highly unreliable,
Gossip is a bane.
But we can't live without it
No matter our disdain.
Innuendo is our Nintendo.
We play it all the time.
So much so, as rumors go,
It really is a crime.

"For You"

"Poem" is a four-letter word
We say all the time.
When we least expect it,
It sounds so sublime.
No matter how you slice it,
I have made a few
But this one is especial.
I made it just for you.

Playing Hooky

I spoke to your mother.
She spoke to your dad,
Who spoke to your teacher,
Who was really mad
That you are a truant.
How will you learn
To think for yourself
And truly discern?

Flippant

We went to the amusement park
Where I nearly died
Slipping and sliding
Down the water slide.
Water slides are dangerous.
If you lose your grip
And start spinning uncontrollably
You may even flip.

Part II

Defiance

Fast makes slow slow
And slow makes fast fast.
Without each other
They would not last.
But me without you
And you without me
Defies all
Possibility.

Desperado

The times, they are a'changing.
They're changing as we speak.
But, for what it's worth,
I am still a freak,
A freak of nature all alone,
By which I mean to say,
A solitary Romeo
No more so than today.

Recherche

Nuclear fission
Is easy to master
Except when it's
A natural disaster
Like for me,
A poetaster,
Accustomed to
Smooth alabaster.

Ambivalence

Charity is love.
Love is war.
This is something
We can't ignore.
But I have heard
It said before
That love is hate
And hate is war.

Chastisements

The corporal kind of punishment
Is a passing fad
Reserved only for miscreants
Who have been very bad.
Time outs can be useful
If you have the time.
But do not underestimate
The benefits of wine.

Superficialities

Beauty is only skin deep.
That's good enough for me.
Appearances can be deceptive.
That's my philosophy.
All that is left
Is our reality.
That is what we call
The things that we can see.

"The Florida Foot"

It is fairly common
For people to use their foot
To push the car door open
Like a mandrake root.
Often this produces
What we call a "ding"
Along with gasps of horror.
That old familiar ring.

Pennies from Heaven

I don't want to die alone
Rotting in this jail.
Do you have it in your heart
To bring to me my bail?
But for them I would not be here.
I am innocent.
And, if perchance you do believe me,
You are heaven sent.

Insouciance

Although my story's often told,
I'll tell you again.
I was once so full of hope.
How quickly did it end.
Hope gave way to sorrow,
Sorrow to despair
Until there came a day
When I did not care.

*Taedium vitae**

I've written my obituary
And my epitaph.
It can be the sort of thing
That really makes you laugh.
You summarize and sermonize
Until they wish you dead.
And so you are, their wish came true.
There's nothing more to dread.

*Latin for "weariness of life."

The Judgment of Paris

Paris was blindsided
By the beauty of Love.
What in the world
Was he thinking of?
Hera and Athena
Could answer this.
Their entreaties
He dismissed.

Atonement

I am Dave, the microwave.
I do my best to behave.
But when will they learn
It's easy to burn?
And yet they always forgave.

A Lethal Combination

I am so blasé.
I can't get out of bed.
And no one can see
What's inside my head.
But this too shall pass.
Just you wait and see.
It's a clinical condition
Fueled by apathy.

Recent History

I would take Hillary in a heartbeat,
Obama on a dare,
Huckabee almost never,
McCain is but a prayer.
What history cannot teach us
We learn from the past:
Winners finish first.
Nice guys finish last.

Sotheby's

Monet and money
Go hand in hand.
The economics of painting
We understand.
When the gardens of Giverny
Are in full bloom,
The auction houses
Are playing their tune.

Work in Progress

Progress is a grand illusion
Based upon the real confusion
That what we see are just delusions
Waiting to be heard.
"Now don't go mixing metaphors.
They will only leave you poor
But never lonely nevermore,"
Said the little bird.

Sunday Mourning

It's birches, birches, birches time.
No, no, no, no churches time.
Birches, birches, birches time.
Birches, birches time.

Encyclical

The world is round.
The square is square.
But there is nothing
To compare
To the shape of things
To come.
The future and the past
Are one.

Apnea!

I woke up this morning
And looked at the clock.
To my surprise
I heard a knock.
It came from the kitchen.
I put on some clothes.
Who could it be?
Nobody knows.

Neverland

As sure as the clock is ticking
Analogically
Willful footsteps quicken
Anagogically
Where to now St. Peter?
We are on our way
To the twelfth of never
Forever and a day.

Cheat Sheet

I found my methodology,
My secret recipe
For making sounds echo
In spoken recitative.
It's really very easy
To make a simple rhyme.
Use a rhyming dictionary.
I do it all the time.

Gabriel

I once kissed the Blarney Stone.
I talk all the time.
I talk and talk and talk some more.
It really is a crime.
Now don't misunderstand me.
It's really not that bad.
I could do much worse
Than have the gift of gab.

Osteoporosis

Books have spines.
People do, too,
Except, of course,
Me and you.
No matter what
People say
We all need
Vertebrae.

The Assignation

Once upon a time
There was a fairy prince
Who left his fairy castle.
They haven't seen him since.
Where would you go
If you were a fairy prince?
"To a fairy princess,"
He said with indifference.

Rendezvous

Although we don't see eye to eye,
We stand toe to toe
And gaze upon the southern sky
With nowhere else to go.
Time passes quickly,
More quickly than you know,
As we wish upon a star
With wild oats to sow.

Always, Sometimes, Never

Always I will love you.
Always I will care.
Sometimes I will forget
That you are always there.
But never will I ever
Forget that you are mine
And that a love like ours
Will stand the test of time.

Deceit and Deception

I rolled back my odometer.
It's against the law.
But I did it anyway.
Winner take all.
I don't have that much to lose
But I have much to gain.
If you don't believe me,
You have half a brain.

Spousal Privilege

The truth is what I say and do
I say and do for you.
But after all is said and done
I know it makes you blue
To think that I have been untrue
And that I don't care
But no matter what I say or do
This is our affair.

The Hanoverian Regression

George succeeded Edward.
Elizabeth succeeded George.
At least they all spoke English
Since the time of Valley Forge.
We are now much wiser
And can truly say
We speak the *King's* English
To this very day.

Bragging Rites

Any braggadocio
Can while away the time
With exploits and capriccios
That make him near divine.
But a man of true integrity
Will always tell the truth
About the things that he once did
In his misspent youth.

Flying Solo

It's as cold as ice, as cold as hell,
As cold as cold can be.
But not as cold as it once was
The day you set me free.
Freedom's just another word
For nothing left to lose.
And it's one thing, in my dreams,
I would never choose.

Elysian Fields

The voice of reason, the voice of God,
The voice inside my head
Tell me I must soon move on
To the City of the Dead.
What could be more natural
Than to breathe our final breath
Contemplating and excoriating
Our unwelcome deaths?

Love Lingers

I told you that I'd never leave
And so you went away
Far from the hustle and bustle,
Far from the general fray.
But mostly you are far from me.
All that I can say
Is that I'd do it all again
If you would only stay.

Quatrain

Like Ike and Mike, we're both alike
But you would never know it.
You're a cad, a lazy lad,
And I am but a poet.

Captains Courageous

A can of beer,
A glass of wine
Make my love
Seem so divine.
Beauty is in
The eye of the beholder
And makes my heart
Grow bolder and bolder.

Part III

Solicitude

I once played the keyboards
In a rock 'n roll band.
I can now hold the keyboard
In the palm of my hand.
Music is universal
When you have two ears
But language is essential
To assuage your fears.

The Rapture

I took the last train for the coast
But when I arrived there
The Father, Son, and Holy Ghost
Had already passed by there.
I turned around to go back home
Not sure of what I'd find there.
It was as if time stood still.
It was the same old grind there.

Penny-wise

When a door closes,
A window opens up.
They will always tell you
To get a signed pre-nup.
If I had a penny
For every time you say
"I will always love you
For now and always…"

Insecurity

With every fiber of my being
I believe it's true.
The heavens and the earth believe it.
Do you believe it, too?
Then why am I uncertain
About what I say and do
And believe with all my heart
That I have been a fool?

Identity

If I were you
And you were me
How confused
We both would be.
But you are you
And I am me.
The rest, they say,
Is history.

Manumission

If perchance you notice
I have gone away,
You may stop and wonder
If I have gone to stay.
If you do not notice,
It is just a well.
Then I will be released
From this prison cell.

Water Proof

Aquafina.
Dasani.
Filtered water
Gets me high.
Now I pray
My soul to keep.
Distilled waters
Run so deep.

On the Rebound

I took it hard when you left.
You might say I was bereft
After the most cruel theft
Of my bleeding heart.
But did you think that I would sigh
Then curl up as if to die
And give it not another a try
When Cupid still has darts?

Cupbearer

The world is spinning 'round and 'round.
I think I'm getting dizzy.
My work is piling up and up.
I hope that I look busy.
But after all is said and done,
All I really need
Is a dose of Dramamine
And a Ganymede.

At the Rainbow's End

The colors of the rainbow
Flashed across the sky
A symbol of God's covenant
That the earth would never die
Until Armageddon,
As John would later reveal
In Revelation 16:16,
The final ordeal.

Catalyst

Biggie likes to eat a lot.
Tabby likes to play.
Biggie is Sir Lancelot
(It's her sobriquet).
Tabby races through the house
In pursuit of Sam
Who thinks that she is being
Chased by a tram.

Freedom

The time is here.
The time is now.
Its time for us
To take a bow.
But when it's time
To leave this stage,
There will be
Another cage.

The Good Die Young.

In due time
You will grow old
Unless you die
Brave and bold.
But, for my part,
I do foresee
That you will live
Eternally.

BlackBerry Jam

I took my time
When I picked you.
How dare you take me
For a fool?
Your credentials were
Impeccable.
You were so
Dependable.

Myopia

If 20/20 is your vision,
There's no need for revision
To look upon the television
In your living room.
But he who sees with deviation
Must soon have the revelation
We require no palliation
When watching cartoons.

Reality Check

Politics and poetry
Are a xenophobic pair.
But when they get together,
Hope is always there.
Their hope is to change the world
One pixel at a time.
Our hope is to save humanity
With one simple rhyme.

A Diet of Worms

One indulgence, two indulgence,
Three indulgence, four—
Martin Luther could not accept
One indulgence more.
He kept on counting until he reached
Thesis Ninety-five.
With all the thunder, it's a wonder,
He made it home alive.

INRI*

It is a fiction that crucifixion
Is ever humane.
All must endure
Excruciating pain.
Humiliation and degradation
Make torture complete
As the cause of civilization
Suffers another defeat.

*Latin abbreviation for *Jesus Nazarenus Rex Judaerum* (Jesus the Nazarene King of the Jews)

"Rivet"

He was walking against traffic
On the shoulder of the road
When somebody hit him
And smashed him like a toad.
What could be more riveting
Than a dying toad
Stopping all the traffic
In the middle of the road?

Taking That First Step

I have always loved you.
And I always will.
I would wait forever.
I am waiting still
To know the measure of your devotion
The fealty of your love.
Must I wait a lonely lifetime
For push to come to shove?

*Chanson de geste**

A poem is a lifeline.
A lifeline is a ship
That sails through the ocean
Just for the fun of it.
But when the fun is over,
If anyone should ask,
What could be more laughable
Than this novel task?

*French for "song of heroic deeds."

Pacifism

The truth is never certain.
Empires do fall.
But the one thing you can count on
Is love can conquer all.
If love is not the answer,
Then what are we here for?
Are we innocent victims
Marching off to war?

Chick Flick

Double is the trouble
When you're Thelma and Louise.
An innocent weekend getaway
Driving in the breeze
Turns into something sinister,
More so as they go.
Two ladies on a joy ride.
Little did they know.

Horace Greedy

Your destiny is manifest.
Your future is clear
As protected by a Doctrine
From our hemisphere.
The exodus was orderly
Until 1849
When California became a state
In a nick of time.

W.C.T.U.*

The experiment was noble
(The results decidedly not).
We drank so much whiskey
Our teeth began to rot.
And when it was over,
The country was besot
Which is why this experiment
Was soon forgot.

*Abbreviation for Women's Christian Temperance Union.

Swansong

Like the swan on the lake
I too must die.
But before I do
I say, "Goodbye"
To the people and places
That I once knew.
But, most of all,
I say, "Goodbye to you."

Urban Legend

I don't know
And I don't care
If you're wearing
Underwear.
If you are,
Good for you.
If you're not,
How do you do?

Renal Failure

I was so pathetic
I took a diuretic
Which is copasetic
To renal functioning.
It left my kidneys very clean
Like a living, waking dream.
I no longer have to glean
Organ trafficking.

Persiflage

A maverick is as marginal
As he dares to be.
A number is an ordinal
In a series
But, in the end, all of this
Really doesn't matter.
What matters is that we indulge
In sycophantic banter.

*Maxima propositio**

Explore, Discover, Learn.
But most of all discern.
If you do,
I will, too.
Explore, Discover, Learn.

*Latin for "the greatest premise."

Sylvan

You can't be entitled
If you don't deserve
The finest education
In a forest preserve
Where there shall be horses
And there shall be boats
And defensive barriers
Controlled by remotes.

Hog Wash

I took it easy.
I took it hard
When I fell in
A tub of lard.
I began to slide
From side to side
But never did I
Lose my pride.

Darwinism

Evolution was a revolution
In our society.
But to simple folk, John T. Scopes
Promoted heresy.
We know now the Mulberg plow
Was a great invention.
But not as great as was the fate
Of the theory of natural selection.

B.F.F.*

When you said you were leaving,
I told you to stay.
When you said you stopped believing,
I showed you the way.
When you look around you
What is it you see?
A culmination of failures
Or do you see me?

*Best friends forever.

He Who Hesitates is Lost.

The time has come
For me to say
"Save it
For another day."
Whatever it is,
It can wait.
But is it wise
To hesitate?

www.ingramcontent.com/pod-product-compliance
Lightning Source LLC
Chambersburg PA
CBHW031216090426
42736CB00009B/941